Little Mitchie

LET'S LOOK INSIDE A BEAVER'S LODGE

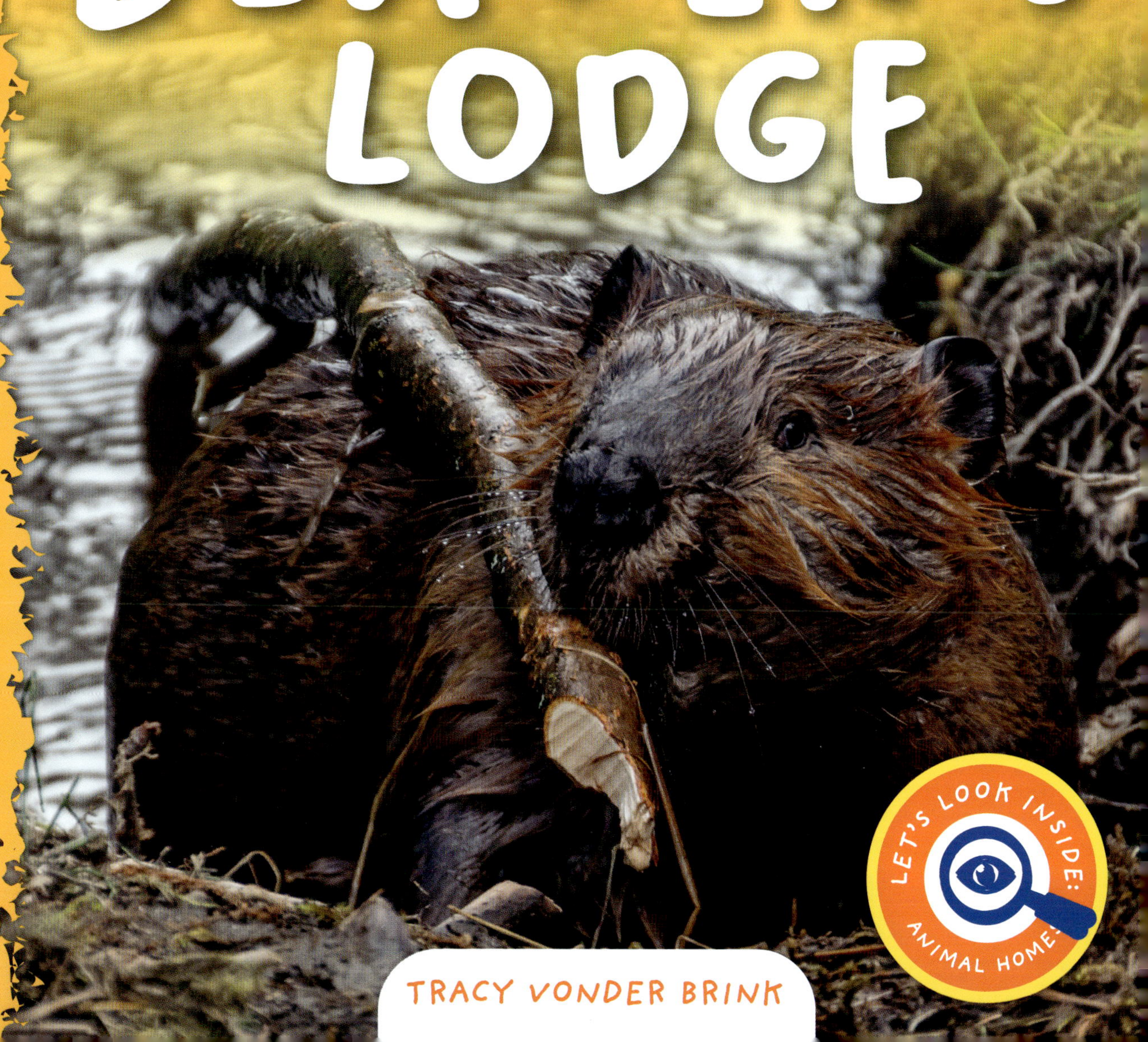

LET'S LOOK INSIDE: ANIMAL HOMES

TRACY VONDER BRINK

CREATING YOUNG NONFICTION READERS

Little Mitchie books spark curiosity and support early nonfiction reading for students in Grades 2-3. Designed to build vocabulary, support second language learners, and prepare readers for middle-grade content, each book includes helpful tips for parents and educators to build confidence and deepen understanding of the world.

TIPS FOR READING NONFICTION WITH BEGINNING READERS

Talk about Nonfiction

Begin by explaining that nonfiction books give us information that is true. The book will be organized around a specific topic or idea, and we may learn new facts through reading.

Look at the Parts

Most nonfiction books have helpful features. Our *Little Mitchie* titles include color photographs and graphic aids, a table of contents, a glossary, and an index. Share the purpose of these features with your reader.

Color Photos and Graphic Aids

A lot of information can be found by "reading" photos, charts, maps, and other graphic aids found within nonfiction texts. Help your reader learn more about the different ways information can be displayed.

Table of Contents

Located at the front of the book, this list shows the big ideas within the text and the page numbers where they can be found.

Glossary

Located at the back of the book, the glossary defines key words and phrases that are related to the topic. These words and phrases can be found in the text in colored type.

Index

Located at the back of the book, an index is an alphabetical list of topics and the page numbers where they can be found.

With a little help and guidance about reading nonfiction, you can feel good about introducing a young reader to the world of *Little Mitchie* nonfiction books.

Little Mitchie is an imprint of:

Mitchell Lane
PUBLISHERS

2001 SW 31st Avenue
Hallandale, FL 33009
mitchelllanepub.com

First Edition, 2027.

Author: Tracy Vonder Brink
Designer: Jen Bowers
Editor: Tricia Hoffman

Library of Congress Cataloging-in-Publication Data
Title: Let's Look Inside a Beaver's Lodge /
by Tracy Vonder Brink

Description: Hallandale, FL :
Mitchell Lane Publishers, [2027]

Identifiers:
ISBN 979-8-89260-872-5 (library bound)
ISBN 979-8-89260-969-2 (eBook)

Library of Congress Control Number: 2026936110

PHOTO CREDITS
Szhutterstock: cover, p.1 ©2018 Jaime Espinosa, p.5 ©2023 VagrantDragon, p.7 ©2017 knik, p.8 ©2020 ebenart, p.9 ©2024 dailymotor, p.10–11 ©2018 Justin Tyler Tate, p.13 ©2024 Tony LePrieur Photography, p.14–15 ©2019 Greenseas, p.16 ©2017 karen crewe, p.18–19 ©2020 Bparsons98, p.20–21 ©2018 Astrid Gast, p.22 ©Nadzin, ©TWINS DESIGN STUDIO, ©jenbowers

TABLE OF CONTENTS

Chapter One

BUSY BEAVERS . . . 4

Chapter Two

PARTS OF A BEAVER'S LODGE . . . 6

Chapter Three

LIFE INSIDE THE LODGE . . . 12

A LOOK INSIDE 22

GLOSSARY . . . 23

FURTHER READING . . . 24

ON THE INTERNET . . . 24

INDEX . . . 24

Chapter One

BUSY BEAVERS

Did you know a beaver's dam isn't its home? Beavers live in a lodge! What is life like inside one?

Chapter Two

PARTS OF A BEAVER'S LODGE

First, beavers make a dam by layering sticks, plants, rocks, and mud. They cut sticks with their sharp **incisors**. Beavers can slice through a tree the size of a person's finger in just one bite!

HOME SWEET HOME

Beavers make a dam first. It slows water and forms a pond, where they build their lodges. Having water all around makes it harder for land predators like wolves to reach the lodge.

Beavers build lodges behind their dams. They use more sticks, rocks, and mud to build a lodge into a **dome** shape. The lodge looks like an island made of sticks. It can be more than 6 feet (2 m) high and 39 feet (12 m) wide.

HOME SWEET HOME

In places where water moves too fast to build a dam, beavers dig a burrow into the riverbank instead of building a lodge. A burrow's entrance is also underwater.

The lodge has underwater entrances. Only something that swims like a beaver can get in!

The entrance leads to tunnels that go up inside the lodge. The tunnels connect to a big room. The feeding **chamber** is near the water. A living chamber is closer to the top.

HOME SWEET HOME

Beavers fill the living chamber's floor with wood shavings to keep it warm and dry. It has a small air hole in its roof. Lodges may also have chambers near the water to store food for winter.

Chapter Three

LIFE INSIDE THE LODGE

Beavers live in a family **colony**. The family is an adult male and female, their young from the year before, and new babies called kits. The whole colony lives in the lodge.

Beavers enter the lodge through the underwater entrance. In the feeding chamber, they dry off. Then, they eat the bark, leaves, buds, and other plant parts they've brought with them.

HOME SWEET HOME

Beavers in the colony spend the fall storing sticks and logs inside the lodge. Then, they can spend the whole winter inside.

HOME SWEET HOME

If the water rises, beavers add more layers to keep the living chamber out of the water. Some lodges can have five or six stories!

Beavers sleep in the living chamber during the day. They also **groom** themselves there. They go down to the water to poop and pee so the lodge stays clean.

In the spring, two to four kits are born inside the lodge. They can swim less than a day later! They practice swimming in the lodge's lower levels, safe from dangers outside. They stay with the family for two years. They help **maintain** the lodge.

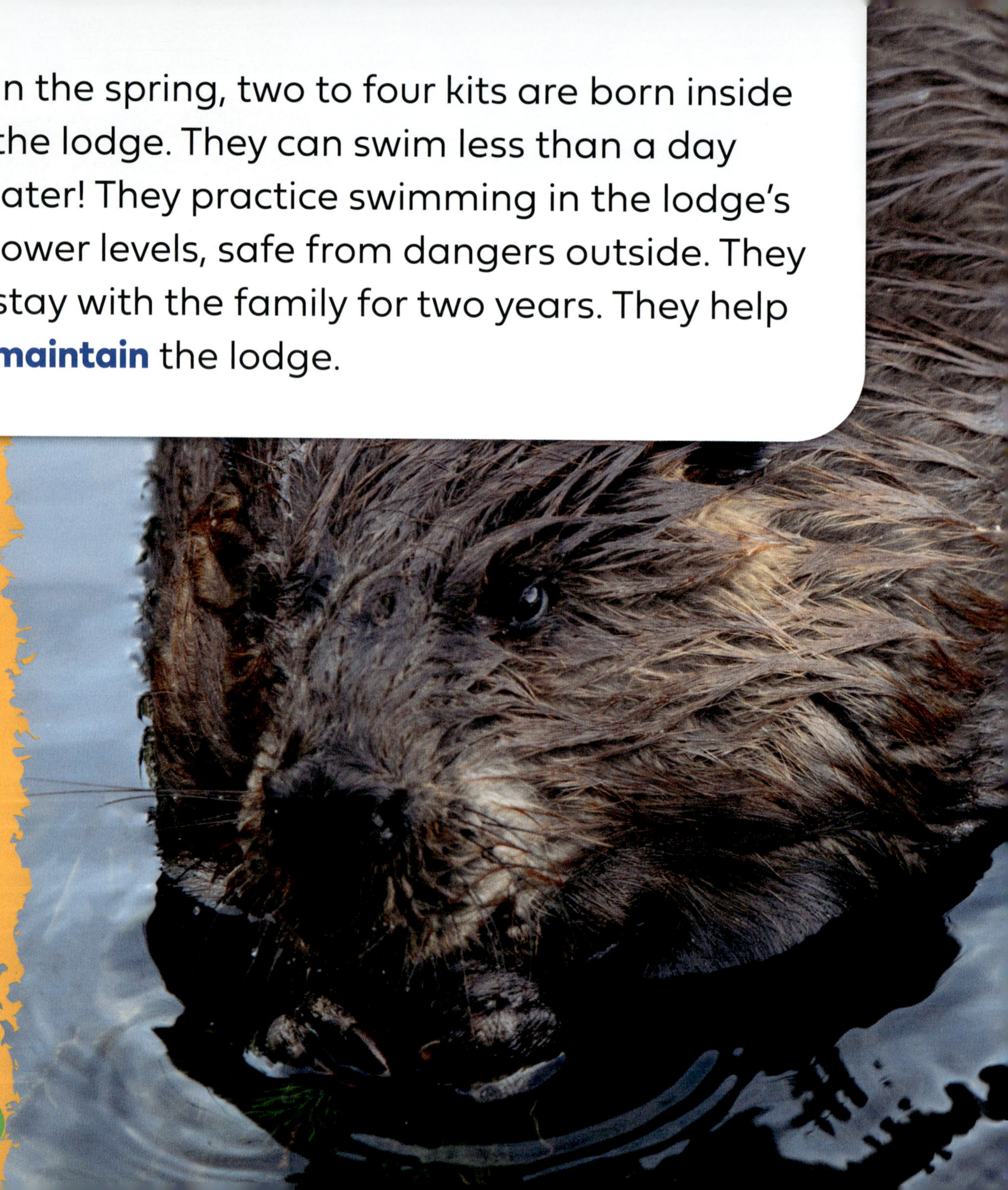

Beaver homes aren't just for beavers! Ponds of water made by beaver dams give beavers a safe place to build their lodges, and they help other animals too. The pools become **habitats** for **wetland** animals like birds and fish.

A LOOK INSIDE

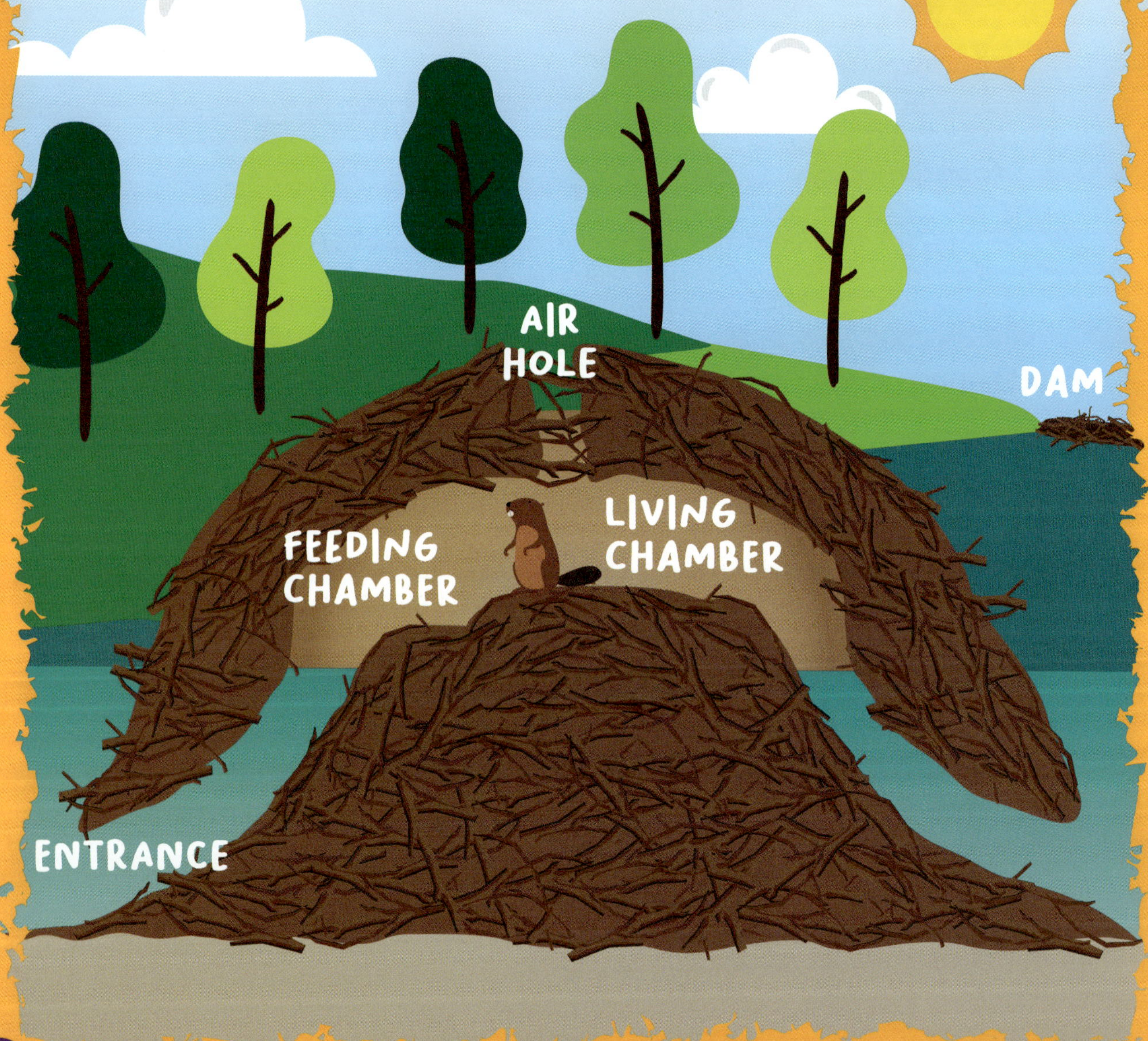

GLOSSARY

chamber (chaym-bur) a room

colony (kah-luh-nee) a large group of animals that live together

dome (dohm) a roof shaped like half of a sphere

groom (groom) to clean an animal's fur

habitats (hab-i-tats) places where animals and plants usually live

incisors (in-sye-zurz) the kind of teeth in the front of the mouth used for cutting

maintain (mayn-tayn) to keep something in good condition

wetland (wet-land) land where there is a lot of moisture in the soil

FURTHER READING

Gop, Becky Cushing. *What Goes on Inside a Beaver Pond?* Storey Publishing, LLC, 2024.

Grack, Rachel. *Beavers.* Bellwether Media, 2020.

ON THE INTERNET

Beaver

https://kids.britannica.com/kids/article/beaver/352837

Find out how many kinds of beavers there are and more with Britannica Kids.

Beaver

https://kids.nationalgeographic.com/animals/mammals/facts/beaver

National Geographic Kids shares facts about beavers and where they live.

INDEX

chamber 10, 14, 16, 17, 22
colony 12, 15
dam 4, 6, 7, 8, 9, 20, 22
entrance 9, 10, 14, 22
incisors 6
kits 12, 18